Explore
FOREST HABITATS
with Grover

Charlotte Reed

Lerner Publications ◆ Minneapolis

There are many habitats to explore!

In the Sesame Street® Habitats series, young readers will take a tour of eight habitats. Join your friends from *Sesame Street* as they learn about these different habitats where animals live, sleep, and find food and water.

Sincerely,
The Editors at Sesame Workshop

Table of Contents

WHAT IS A HABITAT?

Let's explore habitats! A habitat is a place where animals live and can find water, food, and a place to sleep. A forest is a type of habitat.

Forests are full of trees!

LET'S LOOK AT FOREST HABITATS

There are different types of forest habitats. Let's learn about temperate, tropical, and boreal forests!

Forest habitats are found all around the world.

Temperate forests have all four seasons: spring, summer, fall, and winter. In the winter, some trees lose their leaves.

In the spring, the trees grow new leaves!

In the spring and summer, deer eat green leaves and fruit off of the trees. In fall and winter, deer eat twigs and branches.

Me love eating fruit too!

Chipmunks gather nuts, acorns, and berries. They keep them in their dens to eat during winter.

A den is a chipmunk's home!

Tropical forests are warm most of the year and get a lot of rain. Kupok trees grow there and can grow very tall.

Kupok trees are much taller than Elmo!

Gibbons live in tropical forests. They swing from branch to branch looking for food.

Gibbons have strong arms to climb trees.

Sun bears also live in tropical forests. They have short fur to help them stay cool in the warmer weather.

Sun bears have a chest patch that looks like a rising sun!

Boreal forests are cold most of the year and get a lot of snow. The trees keep their leaves all year. Moose live in boreal forests.

Moose's hooves are like snowshoes and help them walk in the snow.

Lynx live in boreal forests too and have long legs that make it easier to walk through deep snow.

I wear my boots when I walk in the snow!

23

The great horned owl also lives in boreal forests. Owls are nocturnal. They sleep during the day and are up at night.

The great horned owl has feathers that look like horns.

Temperate, tropical, and boreal forests are home to many plants and animals.

I love learning about forest habitats!

CAN YOU GUESS?

1. Which of these pictures is of a forest habitat?

A

B

2. Which of these animals lives in a forest habitat?

A

B

Glossary

gather: to get things from different places and bring them together

nocturnal: an animal that sleeps during the day and is active at night

seasons: periods of a year such as spring, summer, fall, or winter

twigs: small branches of a tree or bush

Can You Guess? Answers

1. A
2. A

Read More

Carney, Elizabeth. *Forest Babies*. Washington, DC: National Geographic Kids, 2023.

Neuenfeldt, Elizabeth. *Forest Animals*. Minneapolis: Bellwether Media, 2023.

Reed, Charlotte. *Explore Rain Forest Habitats with Abby*. Minneapolis: Lerner Publications, 2024.

Photo Acknowledgments

Images used: K. D. Kirchmeier/Getty Images, p. 1; Perry van Munster/Alamy, p. 5; bogdanhoria/Getty Images, p. 6; Andrey Danilovich/Getty Images, p. 7; OljaSimovic/Getty Images (right), p. 7; Espair/Getty Images, p. 8; kato08/Getty Images, p. 9; JMrocek/Getty Images, p. 10; Nekan/Getty Images, p. 13; Teo Tarras/Shutterstock, p. 14; Riki Rahmansyah/Getty Images, p. 17; sirichai_raksue/Getty Images (back), p. 18; Bkamprath/Getty Images (left), p. 20; Arman Fazlic/Getty Images (back), p. 20; rpbirdman/Getty Images, p. 22; cindylindowphotography/Shutterstock, p. 24; Mark Newman/Getty Images, p. 25; Karel Bock/Shutterstock (left), p. 26; GUDKOV ANDREY/Shutterstock (back), p. 26; Wirestock/Getty Images, p. 27; laughingmango/Getty Images (left), p. 28; joseh51camera/Getty Images (right), p. 28; Sergey Uryadnikov/Shutterstock (left), p. 29; Stuart Westmorland/Getty Images (right), p. 29.
Cover: Wild-Places/Getty Images; bgsmith/Getty Images; Ukususha/Getty Images; GUDKOV ANDREY/Shutterstock; Ondrej Prosicky/Shutterstock.

Index

For my father, whose fearlessness and stories about gorillas inspired my love of adventure

Lerner Publications Company
An imprint of Lerner Publishing Group, Inc.
241 First Avenue North
Minneapolis, MN 55401 USA

For reading levels and more information, look up this title at www.lernerbooks.com.

Main body text set in Mikado provided by HVD.

Library of Congress Cataloging-in-Publication Data

Names: Reed, Charlotte, 1997– author.
Title: Explore forest habitats with Grover / Charlotte Reed.
Description: Minneapolis : Lerner Publications, [2024] | Series: Sesame Street habitats | Includes bibliographical references and index. | Audience: Ages 4–8 | Audience: Grades K–1 | Summary: "Head into the forest with Grover and the rest of the friends from Sesame Street. Young readers will learn more about the different types of forests and the animals that live in them"– Provided by publisher.
Identifiers: LCCN 2023006044 (print) | LCCN 2023006045 (ebook) | ISBN 9798765604281 (library binding) | ISBN 9798765617465 (epub)
Subjects: LCSH: Forest animals—Habitations—Juvenile literature. | Forest ecology—Juvenile literature. | BISAC: JUVENILE NONFICTION / Science & Nature / Environmental Science & Ecosystems
Classification: LCC QL112 .R444 2024 (print) | LCC QL112 (ebook) | DDC 591.73–dc23/eng/20230424

LC record available at https://lccn.loc.gov/2023006044
LC ebook record available at https://lccn.loc.gov/2023006045

ISBN 979-8-7656-2484-5 (pbk.)

Manufactured in the United States of America
1-1009565-51415-6/21/2023